Alligators

Leo Statts

abdopublishing.com

Published by Abdo Zoom™, PO Box 398166, Minneapolis, Minnesota 55439. Copyright © 2017 by Abdo Consulting Group, Inc. International copyrights reserved in all countries. No part of this book may be reproduced in any form without written permission from the publisher. Abdo Zoom™ is a trademark and logo of Abdo Consulting Group, Inc.

Printed in the United States of America, North Mankato, Minnesota
062016
092016

Cover Photo: Arto Hakola/Shutterstock Images
Interior Photos: Eric Isselee/Shutterstock Images, 1; Raffaella Calzoni/Shutterstock Images, 4; David Osborn/Shutterstock Images, 5; Rudy Umans/Shutterstock Images, 6; Shutterstock Images, 7; AG Technology Solutions/Shutterstock Images, 8–9; No Limit Pictures/iStockphoto, 10–11; Red Line Editorial, 11, 20 (left), 20 (right), 21 (left), 21 (right); Robert Blanchard/iStockphoto, 12; iStockphoto, 13; J. Willis Photography/iStockphoto, 14–15; John Cawthron/Shutterstock Images, 15; Heiko Kiera/Shutterstock Images, 17; Orhan Cam/Shutterstock Images, 18

Editor: Brienna Rossiter
Series Designer: Madeline Berger
Art Direction: Dorothy Toth

Publisher's Cataloging-in-Publication Data
Names: Statts, Leo, author.
Title: Alligators / by Leo Statts.
Description: Minneapolis, MN : Abdo Zoom, [2017] | Series: Swamp animals |
    Includes bibliographical references and index.
Identifiers: LCCN 2016941159 | ISBN 9781680792065 (lib. bdg.) |
    ISBN 9781680793741 (ebook) | ISBN 9781680794632 (Read-to
me ebook)
Subjects: LCSH: Alligators--Juvenile literature.
Classification: DDC 597.84--dc23
LC record available at http://lccn.loc.gov/2016941159

Table of Contents

Alligators

Alligators are reptiles.

They have thick skin.
Their bite is strong.

Body

Alligators can be brown or black.

They have webbed feet. This helps them walk through mud.

They have
strong tails. The tails
have black stripes.

They use their tails to swim.

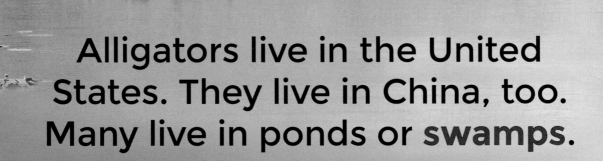

Habitat

Alligators live in the United States. They live in China, too. Many live in ponds or **swamps**.

Where alligators live

Food

Alligators often eat
birds and fish.

They hide in the water
to catch their prey.

They float near
the top of the water.
They wait for hours.

Then they bite their prey.

Life Cycle

Female alligators
lay eggs in nests.

Babies hatch from the eggs
after 60 days.

They stay with their mothers for two years. Alligators can live up to 50 years in the wild.

Average Length

An alligator is longer than a sofa.

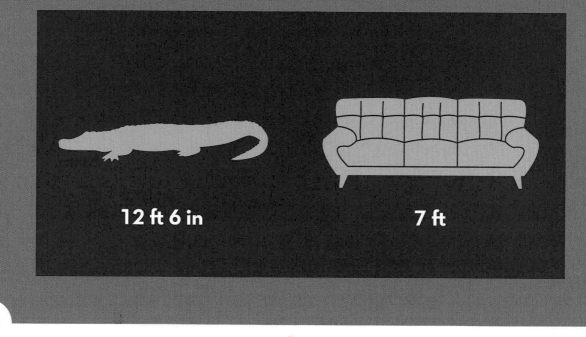

12 ft 6 in   7 ft

Quick Stats

Average Weight

An alligator is almost as heavy as a soda vending machine.

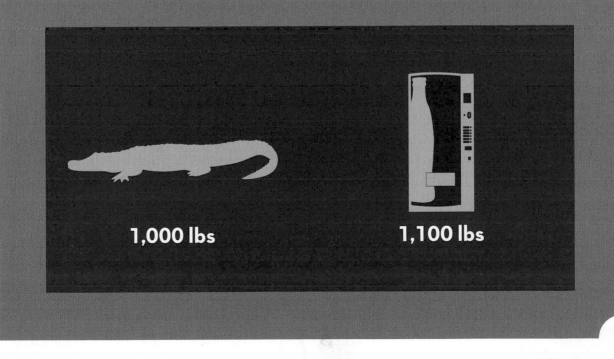

1,000 lbs   1,100 lbs

Glossary

hatch - to be born from an egg.

prey - an animal that is hunted and eaten by another animal.

reptile - a cold-blooded animal with scales. They typically lay eggs.

swamp - wet land that is filled with trees, plants, or both.

webbed - joined together by skin, like the toes of a duck or frog.

Booklinks

For more information
on **alligators**, please visit
booklinks.abdopublishing.com

Z⌕m In on Animals!

Learn even more with the Abdo Zoom
Animals database. Check out
abdozoom.com for more information.

Index